RACE to the
FROZEN NORTH

RACE to the FROZEN NORTH

THE MATTHEW HENSON STORY

CATHERINE JOHNSON

With illustrations by
Katie Hickey

union
square
kids

NEW YORK

To Elsa, the best dog in the world, who let me stay in her house while I wrote this book

**union
square
kids**

NEW YORK

UNION SQUARE KIDS and the distinctive Union Square Kids logo are trademarks of Union Square & Co., LLC.

Union Square & Co., LLC, is a subsidiary of Sterling Publishing Co., Inc.

Text © 2018 Catherine Johnson
Cover illustration © 2024 Hanson Akatti
Interior illustrations © 2018 Katie Hickey

First published in Great Britain in 2018 by Barrington Stoke Ltd. First published in the United States and Canada in 2024 by Union Square Kids.

ISBN 978-1-4549-5485-9

Library of Congress Control Number: 2023942895

For information about custom editions, special sales, and premium purchases, please contact specialsales@unionsquareandco.com.

Printed in China

Lot #:
2 4 6 8 10 9 7 5 3 1

12/23

unionsquareandco.com

Cover photograph of Matthew Henson courtesy Wikimedia Commons; cover design by Melissa Farris

Union Square & Co.'s EVERYONE CAN BE A READER books are expertly written, thoughtfully designed with dyslexia-friendly fonts and paper tones, and carefully formatted to meet readers where they are with engaging stories that encourage reading success across a wide range of age and interest levels.

CONTENTS

INTRODUCTION

Matthew Henson was the first American to reach the North Pole. That was over a hundred years ago in 1909. The American government gave everyone who came home from that trip medals. They were heroes! Did I say everyone? Matthew did not get a medal like everyone else. He did not get a hero's welcome. In fact, for many years some people didn't even believe what he'd done.

Oh, he'd lived a long life, and an exciting one. He'd traveled the world and spoke many different languages. Matthew could drive a team of dogs across the ice, hunt wolves and seals, and make just about anything out of wood or metal.

But when he came home to the land where he was born, the only work he could find was as a messenger boy or parking cars.

He died poor. Only his family and a few others knew about his adventures. But thirty years after he had died, people began to talk about him. They knew the stories were true and eventually he was reburied in a hero's grave. They told his story and remembered his name. Nowadays you'll find schools and colleges and even battleships named after him.

Why was he forgotten and ignored for so many years?

The reason was the color of his skin ...

PART ONE

Running Away

CHAPTER 1

I walked out of my stepmother's house not long after my eleventh birthday. Truth was I'd have left a whole lot sooner if she hadn't beaten me so hard I couldn't get out of bed for three whole days. My stepmother was called Nellie, and she hated me. She had this stick cut from a tree out by our small fields—black oak, I think it was. It was harder than hell and had sharp points that cut into my skin. I don't know what I did to make her hate me so. All I know is that she never beat my sisters half as much as she beat me.

It was always my fault. That last time it was because I filled up the bucket too full with water from the creek. It slopped over the floor in the kitchen. The stick came down hard on my back, arms, legs, again and again. It felt as if every bone in my body was breaking. You should have seen the bruises! My one good jacket got torn.

I had to crawl back up the stairs to my bed and I lay there shivering. It was wintertime and the heat from the fire downstairs only just made it up through the boards. I lay there and looked up at the ceiling. It hurt so bad. That was when I made my mind up to escape.

The first time, I crept downstairs when the house was dark and still, but my bare feet thumped too loud on the stairs and Nellie caught me. She shot out of her bedroom and screamed, thinking I was stealing food. As soon as I saw her reach for that stick of hers, I was back upstairs faster than a squirrel up

a tree. I lay back down in bed with my heart hammering in my chest.

I knew I couldn't stay. I had my mind set on the big city, Washington, D.C. Maybe somewhere there a boy like me could get a job. Had to be better than this. I'll try again tomorrow night, I said to myself. And she won't hear me next time.

I tore up my thin wool blanket into squares. I planned to tie them around my feet so no one would hear me come down the stairs.

Next morning, my sister Eliza looked hard at me. And when Nellie sent us out to cut wood, Eliza told me she'd seen the blanket all cut up. She knew what I'd done that for.

"I have to go," I told her. "Next time Nellie could break my legs."

When we were out of sight of the house, Eliza hugged me tight. "I know, Matt," she whispered. "I thought she'd kill you last time. But I'll miss you so bad."

I nodded. "I'll miss you too. But I can't stay here any longer."

"You going to the city?" Eliza said. "Washington?"

I nodded again.

"Quickest way is up the road past Port Tobacco. I heard people say you can walk there in a day or two," she told me.

I wiped my face with my sleeve. I was sad to leave my sister but I didn't want her to see me cry.

"Always be polite, Matt, and be kind. You'll find work somewhere," Eliza said, and picked a bit of dust out of my hair. "Just you watch out in the city. And remember, when you walk down those big city streets, keep on the outside of the sidewalk, near the road. I heard there's monsters living in those basements. They live in the dark and swallow up colored children who fall in. So you make sure you don't."

I made a face. "Eliza, that's just stories," I said.

"Just stay safe, you hear?"

*

That night I stepped quiet as a polecat down the stairs and across the parlor to the front door. I opened it real slow. I held my breath but the door made no sound at all. Outside, it

was dark and cold. The stars shone like bright diamonds in a great bowl of black, with the moon hung high like a big silver dollar. The ground sparkled with frost, and my breath made great clouds of smoke in the frozen air.

I ran across the moonlit fields and all the way to the road. With every step I took, I was farther away from Nellie and I felt a little bit more free. It was like the stories I'd heard of slaves escaping, and I was setting out toward freedom. I knew if Nellie caught me, she'd drag me back and beat me until she broke my arms and legs.

I could feel the cold, crisp frost through the blanket squares around my feet, but I kept running. When I could run no more, I stepped off the road and into the woods. I pushed some dead leaves out of the way and curled up in a hollow at the bottom of a tree. I held my

jacket tight shut to keep out the chill, but I couldn't sleep, not a wink. I was too cold and too scared. I thought of all those stories I'd heard of night riders. My father used to tell me how they'd come galloping through the dark, hunting down colored folk. They carried flaming torches and their cloaks flowed out behind them. They would shoot you or hang you from a tree just for talking to a white person. Or maybe my cruel stepmother would come hunting me through the woods with her black oak stick in her hand.

As soon as it was light, I set off again. I stayed close to the trees and as I walked I clapped my arms against my side and tried to think of good things. I thought about the times when my daddy let us play with the dog next door. Or when he'd dig a pit and fill it with fire and we'd roast corncobs and sweet potatoes too hot to hold.

I shut my eyes and remembered how warm the food was and how the potatoes were sweet in my mouth. I was very hungry.

Washington will be full of stalls stacked high with oven-hot corncobs or roasted nuts or apple pie, I thought. Then I remembered I didn't have a nickel. Not one cent.

But I couldn't stop now. A big city like Washington, D.C.? I said to myself. There'll be nickels and pennies just dropped in the street, maybe dimes even. After all, didn't the president of the whole of our country live there?

*

I was at the edge of the city by the afternoon. Could smell it a mile off—a thousand chimneys or more smoking with a thousand wood fires. I could see it too—lamps lit in the buildings and on street corners. I wished I could tell someone

what I was seeing—more buildings than I'd ever seen in my whole life, all squeezed up together, and bright yellow gaslight to make the night seem like day. I walked past houses all stuck together in rows with not a bit of grass to be seen. And I saw the basements Eliza told me about, with dark steps leading down into the dark under the houses.

I rushed on even though my feet were sore and I was so hungry my insides hurt.

I stopped outside a house, out of breath, bent double. I heard the door open and a woman cussed at me and told me to get off her property.

Then I found an alley by the side of a church and hunkered down in the doorway. I hugged myself to keep warm. The ground was hard, but I shut my eyes tight and thought about the

summer so as to keep me warm. I was almost asleep when something sharp dug into my side.

"Get out of it, boy!" A policeman stood over me. He must have kicked me in the ribs. I couldn't see his face, because it was dark. But I could see he was swinging a stick, and it was thicker than my stepmother's.

"Did you hear me, boy?" He kicked out at me again and I got up, even though I was still in pain, and ran.

I nearly ran straight down into one of them basements there and then. What would be worse? If I was eaten alive, at least I wouldn't be cold and hungry anymore. I leaned over the railings and looked down. It was so dark I couldn't see a thing. Eliza had been right, I thought. There could be anything down there. The steps could take me straight to hell.

Then I jumped a mile. Something moved. Was it a monster? Suddenly a crack of light opened up—a door, not hell! And a man looked up at me. My mouth must have fallen open, and I froze solid. He came up those steps and I saw then that he had a shovel. I expected him to swipe me hard with it and send me back to Nellie.

"You stealing something, boy?" His voice was a deep growl. Maybe he was a monster in a man's shape.

"No, sir. Never." I pulled my jacket around me and tried to stand up straight. My feet were so wet and cold they hurt like fire.

He looked at me, up and down, and shook his head.

"You a runaway?"

I looked away. I didn't want to answer.
I started to hobble down the street.

He shouted out to me. "Get yourself to
Janey's Cafe. Take a left and it's two blocks
from here. If you're hungry, she might help.
Can't promise ..."

I turned to say thank you but the man had
vanished and I was alone in the cold street.
What if he really was a monster sending me to
my death? But my feet hurt all the way up my
legs and I could feel my hunger fierce inside
me. I had nothing much to lose. So I hobbled
left, counted two blocks, and found a street
with old houses and shut-up shops. Which one
was Janey's? Some of the houses had signs,
but I didn't know my letters other than *M* for
Matt and *E* for *Eliza*. And away from the street
corner the gaslight was dull and I couldn't see
a thing.

But I could smell, and I reckoned I could smell food. So I followed the smell and curled up on the wooden step of a shut-up, beat-up old house.

I was so tired, but I couldn't sleep. I was so cold my teeth rattled in my head. Somewhere I heard a dog bark and a baby cry. Then on a road a ways off I heard the sound of a horse and cart, and I drifted off to sleep as the hoofbeats clip-clopped into the distance.

CHAPTER 2

I must have fallen asleep. The next thing I knew was someone was yelling at me.

"What you doing there?" a woman shouted as she stood over me.

I almost jumped out of my skin! Was she going to hit me? But I must have been dreaming of bacon, because I could sure smell some cooking.

The woman was as wide as she was tall. She had a red-checked scarf around her head and an apron pinned tight across her clothes.

"Nothing, ma'am. Nothing at all, ma'am. Not stealing nothing." I tried to stand, and pulled myself up on the doorframe, but my feet were numb and my back hurt from sleeping curled up like a pill bug. I looked down at the blanket squares around my feet and I saw her look too. I tried to tidy myself up but it was no good. I was a mess—a skinny kid with nappy hair, thin jacket, and trousers almost as muddy as my raggedy old feet.

I felt ashamed. "I'm sorry, ma'am." I said. I could hear bacon cooking somewhere inside that cafe. It was fizzing and popping. The woman frowned at me. Then suddenly she took out a broom. Its long bumpy handle was just like Nellie's stick. I stepped back.

"I don't want no boys sleeping on my step, doing nothing," the woman said. "Can you use one of these?" she asked me.

She held the broom out, not like she was going to hit me after all but like she wanted me to take it!

"Only I need a good deal of help around here. Sweeping and washing up and the like. I could use a hardworking boy." She smiled at me and I smiled right back.

"Yes, ma'am!" I stepped up to take the broom out of her hands.

"Hold your horses, young man!" she said. "First I need to know your name."

"Matthew," I told her. "My name is Matthew Henson, ma'am. I got no folks and ..." I reached for the broom again. "Ma'am, I can sweep your floor so clean ..."

She laughed then. "My name's Janey Moore. This here's my place, best Home Cooked Meals Cafe in town."

She handed over the broom and even though I hurt all over I started to sweep harder than I ever swept in my whole life. Janey put a hand on my back. It was warm. "You can finish that up later. I lived a lot of years and I know a hungry boy when I see one," she said.

She sat me down, and in two minutes there was the biggest plate of bacon and eggs put right in front of me. I don't think I ever tasted anything as good as that first breakfast—the crispy sweet bacon, the dripping yellow eggs. I tried to think about every mouthful but the truth was I shoveled that down faster than a rat runs down a pipe.

Before I'd finished, two old men came
in and sat down. They took one look at me
and laughed.

"Janey," they said. "You gone done took in
another stray?"

"Take no notice of Jack and Moses!" Janey
said. "They just jealous 'cause you got the first
bacon of the day ..."

And that's how I got my first job. Janey let
me sleep under the counter in the cafe and I
did what work I could. Washed up, swept, ran
errands. And Janey said she never knew a boy
work so hard, so she paid me too. And because
I got all the food I needed, I saved the money
she gave me. First thing I bought? A pair of
boots—those fancy ones with brass toecaps. I
thought I was smarter than a brand-new day!

But the best thing about Janey's? The people. Janey's cafe was in a poor part of town but we served all sorts of folk. Young ones on their way to work, old folk with no one at home to cook for them.

My favorite customer was one of the first I ever met, Jack. He was the one who saw me polish off four eggs and so much bacon that if you'd laid the rashers end to end, they'd have reached from Washington to Port Tobacco, Maryland, and back. His name wasn't just Jack. It was Baltimore Jack and Baltimore's the seaport for the great city of Washington. He had some tales. I could listen to him all day. I always swept closer to where he was talking so I could listen, and when I had my own lunch I sat down at his table.

If you looked at Jack, you'd see a broken-down colored man with gray eyebrows,

a face that creased up when he laughed and only just enough teeth to still be able to eat. But the stories he told! Baltimore Jack told me he'd sailed around the world almost as often as I'd had hot dinners.

"I was born in slave times, young man!" He'd say this every time. I didn't like to tell him that I knew some folk only a year or two older than me who were born into slavery and had been sold away from their families. And I knew from stories from my pa—who was born free—that slavery times were the worst for us. But I didn't say a thing. I looked over at Janey and she gave me a smile, so I pulled out a chair so I could listen to Jack talk.

"You want to hear about when I ran away to Cuba? About freedom? About the gold?"

I nodded.

"About riding the waves clean across
the world?"

I sat down.

Baltimore Jack rubbed his chin and let
out a massive long sigh as if talking about his
adventures was the last thing he wanted to do
right now.

"And the whales and the flying fish, sir!"
I said.

"Flying fish? Oh, yes!" he chuckled. "When
I was on deck, whole shoals of them, shining
silver, would come up clean out of the water
and fly over my head."

I shut my eyes for a minute as the old man
talked about the sun on his back and the fish
and the deck that shifted and rolled under his

feet. I almost heard the creak of the wood and the snap of the great canvas sails.

As he told his stories, it was as if I was there on the beach next to him as he pulled up the rowboat. There were brightly colored parrots and tiny hummingbirds no bigger than your finger. There was fruit that tasted sweeter than sugar, hanging off the trees ready to eat.

I leaned forward as he told me how the crew of the *Mary Anne*—his ship—were ready to fight over pirate gold.

Those stories got under my skin and inside my heart. I would lie down on the little bed under the counter and pretend I was on a ship. Baltimore Jack said the sea rocked the ship like a baby in a cradle. So I'd shut my eyes tight and think about the whole cafe set adrift on that wide blue ocean. Swinging me to sleep.

CHAPTER 3

Winter turned to summer, and I washed up and swept, and Janey fed me and looked after me as if she was my mother. My real mother died when I was a baby and I had no picture of what she looked like. Maybe she'd been a bit like Janey? I hoped so.

But I soon started to get restless.

Was I going to spend my whole life sleeping in the back of the cafe and cleaning dishes? If I'd walked all the way to Washington, D.C., from the farm, couldn't I get to Baltimore? Jack had said a hundred thousand ships tied up at the dock there every day. One of them might need a boy. Couldn't I sail the world like him?

One evening, Janey came up as I leaned on my broom. I was dreaming about the wind in my face and dolphins around my boat.

"Matt! You'll dream your life away if you're not careful. Floor won't sweep itself," she said.

"No, ma'am." I started to sweep again.

"You know, you're a good boy, Matt, a hard worker."

"Thank you, ma'am."

"I think you can call me Janey. Everyone else does."

"Yes, ma ... I mean, Janey."

"Now, do you have something to say? Cause I notice you spending more and more time with

your head in the clouds, dreaming your life away . . ."

I froze. I couldn't lie. And it felt like she could read the truth right off my face. "I want to go to sea, Janey . . ." I felt ashamed to tell her I wanted to leave. After all she'd done for me.

She shook her head. "Baltimore Jack been filling your head with stories?"

"I want to see the world!" I told her.

Janey sat me down. "You shouldn't listen to Jack," she said. "He's an old fool. Farthest he ever went on a boat was Boston, up the coast, delivering cotton and hogs. He's telling you about what he wanted to do! Not what he really did."

Her eyes were sad. I didn't want to hear it but I knew she was telling me the truth.

I started to sweep again. I felt angry. Had Baltimore Jack been lying about everything? Was I so stupid to believe it all? "I knew that!" I blurted out. "Spanish gold, flying fish. How could fish even fly?"

"Oh, the flying fish. They are real," Janey said. "I heard of them."

I stopped sweeping and looked at her. "I don't care if half of it is made up! I want to sail the seas! I want to see everything!"

Janey shook her head and I went to bed. But next morning, Janey told me that if I wanted to go I should go, or that wanting would eat me up. She warned me to be careful. She told me there were folk out there who'd treat me badly.

I told her I knew that. Hadn't my stepmother hit me so hard I couldn't walk?

"You're going to have to work three times as hard as anyone else, you hear me, Matt?" She frowned. "You're colored and you're still a child. Plus you got no mama or papa to fight for you," she said.

"I'll work harder than ten boys, Janey, I will!" I said. And I meant it.

She cracked a smile then and made me promise to be good.

*

I spent my savings on a proper suit—well, I thought it was proper even if the pants were a little short—and I polished up my brass-capped shoes till they shone.

The day I left, Janey gave me a whole dollar and a packet of bacon sandwiches. I hugged her tight and, no lie, she wiped away a tear. I felt sorry for leaving her but I would not change my mind. I was too excited.

Baltimore Jack wished me luck. He gave me an address too, of a company that might take on a boy such as me. He told me to head for Fells Point or East Baltimore. The white folks had the west of the city, he said, and I was to keep away from them.

PART TWO

At Sea

CHAPTER 4

I was a very different boy when I left Washington, D.C., from when I first arrived there. I was taller and I had money in my pocket. It was summer but there was some rain, and by the time I reached the port of Baltimore after a day and a half of walking, my suit was dirty and the brass toecaps on my boots were muddy and dull.

I could smell the sea before I saw it. I could smell the smoke and dirt of the city of Baltimore too, but underneath that there was something else—an odd saltiness I could almost taste. It was the sea, bigger and wider than any land, and back then I began to feel as if the whole world was open in front of me.

I had the address that Baltimore Jack had given me. It was a boatyard owned by colored folk who might give me work. I couldn't read the paper Jack had written on but I showed it to a kind-looking shopkeeper who showed me where the Kennard Wharf Chesapeake Marine Railway and Dry Dock Company was.

I walked down to the shore. I could hardly believe what I saw. There were so many boats, it looked as if there was another city out over the sea. The masts of those massive sailing boats stuck up like a forest of trees.

I made my way down to the dockside. Everyone was busy and there was such a crowd of people. Men talking in languages I couldn't understand. Colored men, white men, men with long hair and some with bright tattoos on their arms, loading and unloading bales of fluffy raw cotton and sweet-smelling tobacco.

The air was full of the strong scent of sugar.
There were whaling ships with harpoons on
their decks. And on the dockside were crates
of live animals—pigs and sheep and cows. I
could have stood there all day and all night
just watching.

And, like I said, there were so many boats!
Surely I'd find one who'd give me a job?

It was late in the evening when I found
Kennard Wharf. When I saw it, I felt as if my
heart had sunk into my boots. The company
Jack had told me about built and fixed boats
and their yard was full of ships being repaired.
I didn't want to spend my life being
a carpenter; I wanted to see the world.

I snuck back to the docks and in through
the gates. It was dark now. How I longed to
run up onto one of the ships and hide there—
stow away, Jack called it. How wonderful to

fall asleep in one part of the world and then wake up somewhere else. I watched and waited but some policemen yelled at me to go home, so I ran off. Where could I go? I didn't have a home.

As it got dark and the dockside became quiet, I stopped by the biggest ship I could find. Its dark wooden walls rose up above me, higher than a house, and I reckoned it would be easy to hide on a boat like that. I checked no one was looking and began to climb up one of the ropes that tied it to shore. It was harder than I thought, and as I made my way up toward the boat I mistakenly looked down. I was over the water. It was dark and deep. I could see a fat dead rat bobbing about. What if there were monsters down there too, like the ones Eliza had told me about? Would they jump up and swallow me?

I was up against the ship when I felt a stone hit me, right on the back of the neck. Then I heard a shout.

"Boy! Get down here, boy!"

A policeman! I heard the hard, sharp sound of his whistle. I scrambled up onto the boat and for a few moments I was aboard that wooden world. I felt the deck under my feet and looked up into the masts and saw the new moon shining like a cut fingernail. Then two sailors smelling of rum and beer and dirt closed in on me. They were both so tall they blocked out the sky.

They grabbed me and called me all the worst names. They said they'd throw me overboard with the rats and the rubbish. I thought that was the end of me. I was so frightened I peed myself.

One of them picked me up by my jacket. It tore as he half carried, half dragged me off the ship by the scruff of my neck with my legs kicking out under me. He threw me off the ship and I landed in a heap close to where the policeman was waiting.

The policeman hit me hard and I ran away as fast as I could. It was dark and the policeman was fatter than a Christmas hog, so I got away and hid in a pile of ropes by a warehouse. What could I do now? Would I have to go back to Washington? What would I say to Janey? It took a long time to sleep with all those questions running through my head.

When I opened my eyes, it was still dark. Every bone in my body hurt. My good jacket was torn up and my shoes were scuffed and muddy. I did not look like a boy you'd want to give a job to on any kind of ship.

But I wasn't going to give up. I was going to get work on a ship no matter what!

I looked around carefully to check for policemen but the dockside was quiet. Even in the early morning the sight of all those tall ships took my breath clean away and I did not want to leave. I told myself if I kept out of the way and stuck to the shadows, maybe I'd have better luck this time.

CHAPTER 5

I stopped by a ship with three masts. It wasn't as big as the one I'd tried to climb on last night and it sat lower in the water. I guessed it was loaded up and ready to sail. Where was she headed? Someplace where parrots filled the sky, I reckoned. I was looking at the nameplate but I couldn't make it out. There were no Ms for *Matthew*, or Es for *Eliza*, or Js for *Janey*. It was a puzzle.

Someone was watching me. A white man, tall, with a white beard and wearing a navy sailor's cap. I froze.

"Didn't mean no trouble, sir," I said, ready to run.

He smiled then. First real smile I'd seen since Washington. His face crinkled up and his eyes were kind.

"Like the look of her?" he said, and walked toward me.

"Oh, yes, sir!"

"The *Katie Hines* is a Baltimore Clipper. Best of her kind," the man said. "But I would say that."

"The *Katie Hines*?" I could see the *K* for *Katie* now. "Is she yours, sir?"

"Well, I am the captain. Captain Childs, son, pleased to meet you." He put out his hand.

I froze. A white man had just put out his hand to shake mine. A ship's captain! Was it a trick? Would he just swing me up and into the water quick as a flash?

He smiled again. My heart was thumping as I shook his hand.

"Well, good morning to you, lad," the Captain said. "May the road rise to meet you . . ."

He let go of my hand, touched the peak of his cap as he nodded, then turned away and walked toward the plank that led up to the boat.

I looked at his back. Called out, "Please, sir! Please, Mr. Captain, sir!"

He looked back. I ran the few steps until I was close enough not to shout.

"Do you need a boy, sir? On your boat?
Only I want to go to sea. It's my greatest wish,
sir." It all came out in a rush. "I want to see the
world, sir, I mean Captain."

He looked at me: the muddy shoes, the torn
jacket. I was a little ashamed but I would not
look away.

"And what do your folks think about this?
Do they know you're here?" he asked.

"I don't have a family, sir. Mother 'n father
both long dead, sir. I walked from Washington,
D.C., to find a ship. I was working in a cafe and
I am a hard worker, Miss Janey Moore says so."
He blinked. "Miss Janey Moore of Janey's Home
Cooked Meals Cafe, sir! Captain, sir!"

He looked at me some more. The smile had
gone. I thought he'd walk away. I stood up as
straight as I could.

"How old are you, boy?" he asked.

"Twelve near enough, sir."

"Can you read and write, boy?"

My heart sank. I looked down at the mud on my brass-capped boots.

"Know anything about navigation or the stars?" he asked.

I felt a lump in my throat the size of a whole apple. Was I ever going to get a job on a ship? I wanted to run away but I made myself look right at the captain.

"No, sir," I said. "I've never been on board a ship yet, but I can clean dishes and scrub and wash anything, and I can sweep floors so hard there's not one speck of dirt or dust left in the whole place. Day or night! You never met a boy could sweep harder than Matthew Henson, sir, Captain, sir."

He put his hand over his mouth. He was trying not to laugh—I could see that.

"I ain't a liar neither," I told him.

He shook his head.

"You know what, Matthew?" he said, and his voice was kind. "I believe you."

"You do?"

"Well, it just so happens the *Katie Hines* needs a cabin boy. We're off across the world, making for Hong Kong—that's in China. It'll take a year there and back. It's all the way across the world," he told me.

I shook my head. Was I hearing right?

"You have to promise me something," the Captain said. "You'll have to do as you're told and work like a demon."

"Oh yes, sir, Captain, sir!"

"There'll be cooking and cleaning aplenty. But you're going to have to learn your letters. Is that clear, son?"

"Anything you say, sir!" I tried to salute. It felt like the very best day of my life.

CHAPTER 6

One short week out of Baltimore and I think I loved the *Katie Hines* just as much as Captain Childs. I worked harder than I'd ever done before, even harder than when my stepmother Nellie made us chop wood all day and all night.

Two months out and I felt I'd found my home, and by six months out I'd found my family. There were men from all over the world on that ship. Pincus was the cook and he was from New Orleans. At first, I spent most of my time with him. He didn't like me to start with, but once he'd seen that I could peel potatoes quicker than anyone, he was happy. The bo'sun, Mr. Hanley, taught me carpentry:

how to make a good square joint and how to put a decent box together. I liked that work a lot!

The first mate, Mr. Tracy, taught me the name of every star in the sky, and there are so many it took a fair long time. He also taught me how to navigate—how to find out the ship's position and to make sure we stayed on course.

I climbed the rigging and washed the decks till my hands were raw, but I saw dolphins and flying fish too, just like Baltimore Jack said. I wished I could tell him and Janey everything I was seeing.

But there was also something else. For an hour every afternoon, Captain Childs taught me my letters, numbers, and history. And while I wrote out my letters, sometimes the Captain would read to me. That was my favorite. He read adventure stories, *Ivanhoe* and *Huckleberry Finn*. History stories, tales about gods and monsters, stories about pirates and sea battles even better than the ones Baltimore Jack told me. And by the time we got to Hong Kong, I was beginning to read them all by myself.

*

The harbor at Hong Kong was different from any of the harbors we'd stopped at on the way. The boats were different for a start. When Captain Childs asked me to go ashore, I was too scared. What if I got lost? What if I never found my way home? I begged to stay on board even when some of the sailors made fun of me.

But the Captain taught me a few words of Chinese—*please* and *thank you* and some others—and that afternoon I stepped ashore. It was like another world. The food and the colors! The sailors from the *Katie Hines* almost all drank themselves stupid but I found a shop that sold tiny songbirds on strings tied around their feet. I would have happily kept one with me on the ship but then I thought of what it would be like to spend your whole life tied down, so I paid for one with my own money and set it free. I watched it fly up over the harbor as the *Katie Hines* set sail for Baltimore again.

I stayed on board and learned and learned. By that time I was thirteen and, because there was no doctor on the ship, it was me who looked after the crew when they were ill. I could make a splint if you had a sprain, or burn out an ulcer with a red-hot pencil.

By the time I was fourteen, I could steer a ship across any ocean and make a good chair and table if you'd need one. I could rig out any vessel you like and I spoke enough Spanish and Russian and Chinese to get by ashore.

But best of all I could read all the books in the Captain's cabin. He'd let me borrow any one I liked and I raced through them.

We sailed to the Caribbean and to the Philippines, beautiful islands with coconut palms on the beach. We sailed to Japan, North Africa, Spain, and France.

When I was fifteen, we sailed to Murmansk, in the far north of Russia. We arrived just as the sea froze, and the *Katie Hines* was trapped there all winter. It was twenty degrees below zero and very dark. Some days the sun only just rose above the horizon.

The Russian sailors knew how to have fun. They taught me to drive Russian ponies that pulled ice sleds across the frozen plains and they took me on my very first wolf hunt.

One day, I thought, I would find Baltimore Jack and tell him about my adventures! But for now, all I wanted was to stay on the *Katie Hines* and see every single country in the whole world.

*

But when I was seventeen everything changed. The *Katie Hines* was heading home to Baltimore from Kingston, Jamaica. We'd been at sea a day. I'd spent my shore leave up in the mountains. When I came back on deck, I'd told the Captain about every one of the hummingbirds I'd seen, and about the waterfall I'd swum in.

The next day, I spent the morning up in the rigging and it wasn't until midday that I thought about how I hadn't seen the Captain on his rounds that morning.

I saw the bo'sun hurry by; his face was set hard. I could see something was up.

"Mr. Hanley!" I shouted. "What is it?"

The bo'sun said nothing. He was heading for the Captain's cabin, so I followed him.

Mr. Hanley pushed open the door without knocking and I saw Captain Childs lying in his bunk. He looked pale as milk, his eyes ringed red. I pushed past the bo'sun and put my hand on the captain's head. It felt like he was burning up.

"He woke up like this," the bo'sun said. "In the grip of the fever."

"You should have told me!" I kept my voice low even though I was angry. "You'll be all right now, Captain," I said, and tried to sound like I meant it.

The fever raged all that day and all night too. The Captain had always looked old to me, but he'd been strong and fit. He worked just as hard as the younger men on board.

But not anymore. Now he looked small and gray, and he only got worse. I searched the ship's medical books but I couldn't find any answers. Nothing I did seemed to help.

After two days, Captain Childs opened his eyes and tried to sit up.

"Matthew!" he said, as if he didn't know I'd been by his bed all that time. "Do your best, son. Never stop learning and growing. Don't let anything get in your way, Matt."

"Of course, Captain, of course."

He gripped my hand. "Life is a journey toward death. Live as well as you can ..."

Then the fever made him shake and he shouted out for water. His voice was a shallow croak. I prayed and prayed for the Captain to live but I knew there was no hope.

We buried Captain Childs at sea and the ship limped home to Baltimore without him. Truth be told, he was more than a captain to me—he'd been like my best friend and my father.

CHAPTER 7

I didn't want to sail on the *Katie Hines* anymore without Captain Childs. And I didn't want to stay on land, so I signed up as an able seaman on another boat out of Baltimore. It was the *White Seal*, a two-masted schooner that was headed to Newfoundland up north to fish for haddock and cod.

I hated life on board the *White Seal*. Our food was dirty herring that looked liked it had been scraped off the ship's hull. On top of that the captain was a drunk. I got off that ship as soon as I could and worked my way back down through Canada to get home. I made a promise to myself that I would live my life just as Captain Childs said—I'd live for adventure and learning and try to see as much of the world as I could. Didn't I have learning now?

But as soon as I reached the United States, I knew my plans would never work. I was a colored man. Many of the white people I met enjoyed making sure that I knew I was the lowest of the low. The only work I could get was as a messenger boy, bellhop, or night watchman. It felt as if those promises I made to Captain Childs had come to nothing. My life might as well have been over. And I was only nineteen.

When I made my way back to Washington, I found that Janey's cafe had closed down in the seven years I'd been away. Someone on the street told me Janey had died. No one had even heard of Baltimore Jack.

I found myself a job in a big store, Steinmetz and Sons, which sold any sort of hat you could think of. Hats for riding the plains of the Wild West. Hats for keeping the rain off in the tropics. Hats lined with fur for the frozen north. The owner, Mr. Sam, was a good man. He was fair and treated me right, and sometimes, when I forgot about the wide world beyond the sea, I enjoyed it.

*

One day, I was sorting new stock in the supply room and life seemed fine. I'd been at the shop for about a year and a half and I longed for adventure, but I now knew how hard it would be for me to go to sea again. There were not many men on this earth like Captain Childs, men who would give a colored man a chance. I knew that now. I remembered how Janey had told me how hard it would be. I thought how lucky I had been that I had already seen so much.

Mr. Sam shouted for me to bring some sun hats onto the shop floor. There, on the other side of the counter, stood a tall white man wearing a Navy officer's dark-blue uniform. There was something about him that made me feel good. Was it that he reminded me of Captain Childs?

I was thinking this when Mr. Sam said, "Here's the boy I was telling you about, Officer Peary."

I didn't like it when people called me "boy." I was twenty-one—wasn't I a man? But I said nothing. There was no point.

"I'm looking for a valet," the Navy officer said. His face was open and honest. "I'm going to Central America and need a boy to look after my clothes. Mr. Sam here says you're a hard worker. The best. Honest too. Just what I'm looking for."

Mr. Sam took one of the sun hats and passed it to Officer Peary. "We'd be sorry to see you go, Matt, but when the officer told me about it I thought of you. To be frank, Matt, you've been the best boy we've ever had working here."

"A valet, sir?" I said to Officer Peary. I did not want to be a valet. A valet's job was to iron and clean clothes. But perhaps if it gave me the chance to travel again it might be worth it.

"Where are you headed, sir?" I asked.

"Nicaragua. It's in Central America, south of Mexico. We're in the advance team for a canal that's going to be cut through the American continent going from the Atlantic Ocean to the Pacific. Our job is to make the charts and see what the land is like. It'll be pretty heavy going. It's mostly jungle. An adventure, I'd swear."

I looked at the man. Perhaps it would be interesting. Peary looked at me.

"What do you say, young man?" he asked.

I smiled. He didn't call me "boy." I nodded. He put out his hand. And for the first time in a long while a white man shook hands with me like an equal.

"I think I'd like that very much, sir!" I said.

CHAPTER 8

We spent seven months in Nicaragua, and
Officer Peary was a good boss. I was happy
with him. After a few weeks, Officer Peary saw
I could pretty much make anything out of wood
that needed making, as well as dig ditches or
clear jungle. He promoted me to the transit
crew, which meant my new job was with the
team of men who took readings to measure
the height of the land above sea level so we
could make maps, as well as dragging heavy
equipment through the jungle. Our team
worked hard together, and I knew I was a part
of something big and exciting.

Officer Peary said he was so impressed
with me that he'd find another job for me once

we returned to America. He kept his promise.
Peary found me work at the League Island
Navy Yard in Philadelphia. It was only as an
errand boy but I worked hard and waited for
something better.

*

I worked at the Navy Yard for a year, fetching
and carrying but always dreaming of adventure.
One day, Officer Peary came to find me.

"Matthew! Matt Henson!"

I heard him shout for me. I was in the
middle of taking a message from one office to
another and I couldn't really stop, but Peary
walked alongside me. His eyes shone as if he'd
just been given the best present anyone could
wish for.

"It's happened at last!" he said. "I've got the leave and I'm going north again!"

"You are, sir?" I didn't understand.

"When you're done with that errand, come to my private office! Right away. We will change the world, Mr. Henson!" he said, and headed off.

I shook my head and went on with my delivery. I didn't know what he was talking about. I remembered the journey to Nicaragua, and the trail we'd carved through the jungle, but I tried not to get too excited.

When I stepped into Peary's office, his desk was empty except for one enormous map spread out like a great white sheet. In fact, at first I didn't know it was a map because it was so white and empty looking.

"Is it another expedition, sir?" I asked. "South America, sir?" I stood opposite him and looked at the map.

"Better than that, Matt. Much better. I've been to the frozen north once before, and every day since I've been trying to put together a team to go back. We'll be away for eighteen months and we will go as far north as any man can go. The north coast of Greenland—high in the Arctic Circle. Maybe even to the farthest north. To the North Pole."

He told me about his journeys to the Arctic, about all he'd seen there: massive icebergs, so white they seemed to shine with a strange blue light, and glaciers—solid rivers of slow-moving ice that creaked and groaned like living things. He said there were places that were dark all winter and where the sun didn't set all summer long.

"I know about the far north, sir," I said. "I've been trapped in ice before. When I sailed on the *Katie Hines*. We spent a winter in the north of Russia—we didn't see the sun for weeks . . ."

"That's it! That's what it's like! And I know you're used to hardship, to struggle. You work as hard as three men. I need someone like you, Matt."

"But, sir, I'm not a scientist or a Navy man."

"Matt, you'd be busy all the time! Building sleds, making stoves, hunting, driving dogs . . ."

"I've never driven dogs, sir."

"I've seen you at work, Matt," he told me. "There's nothing you can't do. This journey will be hard, sledding through ice and snow.

There'll be plenty of danger too. Out on the ice. We'll need someone like you—who's tough and likes a challenge." He looked back down at the map and his fingers traced the edges of Greenland and Ellesmere Island.

I looked at the vast white shapes and thought of the bears and the wolves and a new world open in front of me.

"Yes, sir," I nodded. It was easy. I wanted adventure. "I'll come."

"There's one big problem, Matt. Money's tight. There's no pay, I'm afraid."

I didn't care. I thought of Captain Childs and what he'd have said. I'd be living one of those adventures I read about in his books. I'd be living!

"If Greenland's as empty as this map," I said, "looks like there'll be nothing to spend any money on up there."

He slapped me on the back and shook my hand. We spent the afternoon together. Peary told me his plans and we made lists of what we were going to need and how we would spend the money we did have. We had to plan with care. Our ship was going to be a steamship, the SS *Kite*. We'd have to buy dogs from the people who live around the northeast coast of Greenland, the Inuit.

Peary told me about the crew he'd already found. Some folk had paid to come along, and others were working for nothing, like me. There was a professional skier from Norway, name of Astrüp; a doctor from Brooklyn, Dr. Frederick Cook; and a young geologist named Verhoeff. A mix of adventurers and scientists.

None of the others, apart from Peary, Astrüp the skier, and me, had ever been to the frozen north before. That far north the temperatures are so low that frostbite can turn your toes and fingers black. The cold kills the nerves and blood vessels and makes your fingers and toes drop off. In Murmansk there'd been men who had lost their noses too. I didn't like thinking about that but I still knew I was doing the right thing.

When some of the other officers at the Navy Yard heard I was going, they teased me. They told me a colored man would die of cold up there in the snow. They said a Negro like me, on account of my coming from somewhere warmer, would fade away. In fact, one of the officers promised he'd give me one hundred dollars if I came back alive and with all my fingers or toes. I told him to start saving.

PART THREE
The Arctic

CHAPTER 9

At last I was going to the Arctic. Our expedition set sail in the autumn of 1890 and we reached the coast of Greenland a month or so later. I must admit I was a little disappointed. Instead of vast plains of white as far as I could see, there were only treeless hills and snow-capped mountains.

As the *Kite* came into port, though, I noticed something that shone from beyond the mountains. A light. What could it be? The sun was behind us. I leaned out over the rail.

Peary stood beside me. "That's iceblink, Matt," he said. "It's the light given off by the polar ice cap. The sun reflects off all the snow. It's almost as bright as a second sun."

I tried to think about what it would be like up there on the ice cap. Was it like a Russian winter, only bigger and colder?

We unloaded the ship. I worked till I was ready to drop. No one else was a carpenter, so it was up to me to build a house and make the sleds. Peary planned the sleds himself. Instead of metal bolts and fixings, the wood was lashed together with walrus skin.

The work was done a few weeks before the real cold weather of winter set in. And it was about this time that a boat came down from Northumberland Island, where some of the crew had gone to trade with the local Inuit. It was carrying a pack of howling, barking sled dogs. I couldn't see how such a wild pack of animals could ever be made to do anything at all. They snapped and yelped, they fought with one another, and they ate everything—even their own dirt.

Then I saw a family get off the boat after the dogs. They were dressed in skins—a man, woman, and two small children. All had straight black hair and deep-brown skin. The man saw me and ran from the jetty where the little boat had docked. He ducked around the yapping dogs, came straight to me, and hugged me as if I was his long-lost brother.

I was a little shocked but tried not to show it. He talked at me in great excitement but I didn't understand a word he said. At last he pulled away from me, but he kept talking.

"I'm sorry, sir," I said, and shook my head. I tried to show him that I didn't understand his language.

He took my arm and pushed up the sleeve of my shirt, and then pushed up the sleeve of his own animal-skin jacket. He put his arm next to mine. Our skin was almost the exact same shade of brown. He looked at me and I smiled.

"You mean we're the same?" I said.

"Same!" he said and nodded. "Same!"

He put his hand flat on his chest, against his heart. "Ikwah," he said. "Ikwah."

Ah! That must be his name, I thought. I put my hand on my chest and said, "Matt. My name is Matt."

"Miy," Ikwah said.

"Close enough!" I smiled and shook his hand. Ikwah hugged me again.

*

He was the first Inuit I ever met, and he became my friend. A few weeks later, a second group of Inuit arrived. They'd come down from a trading post where the crew had traded guns and needles, pots and pans, for furs and more dogs.

This was when I met Ahnalka. He was unloading the dogs with Ikwah. I tried to talk to them with the few words I'd heard. I made hand signals to try to ask them to teach me how they fished. I had seen the Inuit fishing through holes in the ice. How did they know where to make the holes? I tried to act out what I meant. I could see Ikwah and his friend Ahnalka laughing at me as I jumped around pretending to catch a fish. I reckoned I must have looked really funny, so I began laughing too.

After that, Ahnalka and Ikwah became my teachers as well as my friends. Every day I learned more of their language, and every day they taught me how to hunt and fish in their frozen country.

I learned how to build stone igloos or, when there was no stone, with bricks made out of ice. I learned how to load a sled and the best way to wear and sleep in your furs, how to pack my sealskin boots with dry moss to keep warm, and how to warm up frostbitten fingers and toes.

It felt a little strange at first, warming ice-nipped fingers in my armpits. If my toes got frostbite, Ahnalka said, I was to take off my boots and put my feet on a friend's bare stomach. I thought of the bet I'd made at home, one hundred dollars, and promised I'd do as they said.

The most important thing they taught me was how to drive a dogsled. What you have to understand is that those northern sled dogs were nothing like the dogs you might find in an American town or on a country farm. These animals were more like wolves. If you wanted to control them, you needed mental power as well as to be strong.

Ahnalka and Ikwah made it look easy. They cracked the long whip made of walrus skin and set the dogs off all at once, speeding over the snow, the dogs running fast and free. But when I tried it, the dogs just sat down and ignored me. Ahnalka and Ikwah laughed for a very long time.

The rest of the crew, even Peary, gave up trying to learn. Peary changed his plans. He decided he'd ask the Inuit to drive the sleds. But I kept on trying. It took weeks to learn to holler the commands exactly the way Ahnalka and Ikwah did. But after trying and trying, I could crack the thirty-foot-long whip behind the lead dog as I shouted out the commands in perfect Inuit.

There is nothing as exciting as driving a dogsled across a clear, snowy plain. There is something magical about all that snow stretching on for miles just like icing on a cake. But there was one problem. Where we were going, the snow and the ice would not be smooth.

The Inuit almost never went out onto the polar ice cap. There was no solid land up there, they told me, only a shifting skin of ice that melts every summer and freezes every winter. It can change or break up overnight. Ahnalka explained there was a devil, an evil spirit, who

lived under the ice cap and who could swallow
people up in one gulp.

Ahnalka told me about pressure ridges too,
where the ice has been forced up into solid
waves that you can't sled over. He also told
me about the leads—stretches of open water
that can suddenly open up in between the ice.
But worst of all, he told me, were the crevasses.
These are bottomless cracks in the ice. If you
fall in one of those, you'll never get out. One
time he'd seen a whole pack of dogs and their
sled vanish into one. The thing about crevasses
is that they are often covered by a thin crust
of fine snow, so you can't see them until it's too
late and you've been eaten alive by the devil in
the ice.

*

That first winter with Ahnalka and Ikwah, I hunted polar bear and wolf, fished through the ice, and tracked caribou for days. Some of the men, Dr. Cook for one, were bad hunters. They scared off the caribou after we'd followed them for a week or more.

But while I became a good hunter, I learned never to kill more animals than you need for meat. To respect every living thing in that harsh, frozen winter land.

*

We set off from camp in June 1891 and our expedition reached the far north of Greenland. Peary said we should make a journey up the glacier and onto the ice cap to see how far we could get. Ahnalka and Ikwah tried their best to persuade us not to go out onto the ice, but Peary told them that was why he was here: to find a way to the North Pole.

The climb up out of the glacier was almost impossible. There were hundreds of pressure ridges and crevasses. They were so deep and dark you could not see the bottom. We managed to avoid them but I saw why you might think there was a devil waiting to eat you whole down there. I remembered what my sister Eliza had said to me all those years ago, about the monsters who wait for you down in the dark.

We traveled north for over a month, then very bad storms blew up that kept us in our igloos and, even worse, the dogs became ill and some of them died. Peary told me he and Astrüp, the skier, would go up onto the ice cap but that I should take the last few dogs back to camp.

Ahnalka and Ikwah were very happy to come back to camp. We waited for the others but days passed and there was still no sign of them.

Verhoeff, the young geologist, was fed up with staying in camp. He'd paid to come on this trip to collect samples. He knew there were meteorites out on the ice cap that had fallen from space, as well as all sorts of interesting rocks and fossils. He was angry. He said he hadn't come all this way to spend the winter cooped up in a tent. I told him he had to wait. I knew he didn't know the frozen north well enough to set out on his own.

Many days later, Peary and Astrüp returned. They were starving and exhausted but Peary was excited. They had traveled four hundred miles out onto the ice cap, farther north than he had ever been.

And now Verhoeff said he had to go and collect rock samples. The *Kite* was due to set off for home, and if he didn't go now, he would miss his chance. I thought it was a bad idea and said so. But Peary was too worn out to put up a fight and Verhoeff took no notice of me.

He never came back. Ikwah and I went to look for him. We followed his tracks through the snow but the trail stopped suddenly by a crevasse. We knew Verhoeff must have fallen into the inky darkness. I called down but there was no trace of him. Ikwah told me the devil had taken him.

Peary blamed himself for letting Verhoeff go off alone. And so, in spite of the expedition going places no one had ever been before, the journey home was gloomy.

As we docked in New York, I was thinking about collecting my hundred-dollar bet, when Peary called me into his cabin. "Astrüp and I got so far, Matt," he said. "I wish you'd come with us. If we'd had the dogs and a good driver like you or Ahnalka, I think we'd have made it all the way to the North Pole."

"Really, sir?" I said. "The North Pole?"

"I believe so, Matt. And I want us to be the first to reach the Pole. I know we can make it!"

I was as excited as he was! How would it be if I was one of the first men to reach the North Pole? I'd make history! How incredible would that be for me? I was a man with no mother or father and nothing of my own. Captain Childs would have been so proud of me.

"I'm not going to stop now, Matt," Peary said. "We know how dangerous it is up there.

I plan to start raising the money right away. And I need you on board. You're the best of the whole damn crew! Are you with me, Matt?"

I didn't need to think about it. "Yes, sir!" I said.

CHAPTER 10

That first trip was the beginning of over nineteen years working with Peary and traveling to the frozen north. We didn't know it then but it would take us all that time and four more expeditions to get to the North Pole.

The second journey in 1894 was the worst. We set out across the ice cap with three sleds and thirty-seven dogs. But we returned with only one sled and one dog. We had to haul our equipment ourselves, and we had to walk for miles through freezing ice and snow. We were starving most of the time and the temperatures were some of the coldest I remember.

Conditions were also hard during our third expedition, which set out in 1898 and lasted for almost five years. One time we were trapped in an igloo for days without food while a wild storm blew outside. Peary became ill, so I sent Ahnalka back to camp to get help. I tried to keep Peary warm under the skins and rugs. From time to time he cried out that his feet were burning away, so I took off his boots to see. He had bad frostbite. As I edged his boot off to look at his feet, nine of his toes, black and rotten, came off too.

When we got back to camp, I was almost dead myself. Ahnalka brought me hot, freshly killed seal's blood, which he said was the best medicine for me. I drank it down and it must have worked. Peary did not want to drink it. He took a lot longer to get better than I did.

Ahnalka saved my life a second time. We were working together on the polar ice cap. Our job was to drag supplies to the next camp, ready for the expedition that would arrive there the next day. Up ahead of us, the ice was white and firm and endless. There were no pressure ridges to struggle over, no leads or stretches of open water. It was a good day. Then suddenly, with no warning at all, the solid ice gave way and opened up under my feet. A crevasse! For a split second I thought I would fall forever. But then Ahnalka grabbed me and we stared into the dark together. Once again, my Inuit brother had rescued me. I would never forget him.

*

With so much danger at every turn, why did I want to go back to the Arctic time after time to risk my life? The answer is that there was something about that empty land with its strange, glowing light—the blue whiteness that sometimes shades into green—that was like nowhere else on Earth. When I got back to America, I missed the friends I had made there. Ahnalka most of all. I knew Captain Childs would have got on with him just fine.

Life for a colored man in the United States of America was never easy. Back home, the sort of jobs I could get were dull and badly paid: delivery boy, errand boy, shop assistant. No matter how many letters Officer Peary wrote to try to help me get more interesting jobs, nothing changed.

Life on the ice was different. People respected me there. I learned more and more about the secrets of that icy world and I was able to teach them to new explorers: how to drive dogs, how to hunt for food and keep warm, how to build shelters in the ice and watch for its dangers. Who wouldn't choose adventure and excitement over a life at home that was hard and unfair?

CHAPTER 11

After the time I had spent near the polar ice cap, with its danger and its beauty, my life back home was sad and dull. I felt trapped. Were my exploring days over? Perhaps I'd never see the north again. My travels to the North Pole seemed like a dream.

At last, in the summer of 1908, Commander Peary wrote to me to tell me he had funds for one last journey. He had the backing of President Theodore Roosevelt himself. If you'd seen me when I got that letter, you might think I was crazy, I was so excited. I danced about my room and I didn't care who saw me.

A few weeks later, I said my farewells and rushed to join Peary's ship. It was called *The Roosevelt*, after the president who had given us money for the trip. Peary was waiting for me on the gangplank.

"It's all or nothing this time, Matt," he said as he shook my hand. "We have to make it."

It seemed to me that Peary's mood was harder since I'd last seen him. It was as if something was eating at him inside.

"And did you hear?" he said. "Dr. Cook is already in Canada and says he is on his way to the Pole. You know who I mean, Matt? He was on our first expedition together, and I don't trust him. He says he's a doctor but I'm not sure. I didn't like the way he treated the Inuit on our first expedition together, and I didn't believe the stories he told us."

"Dr. Cook won't bother us," I told Peary. "That man won't last a minute on the ice, believe me. He's a terrible hunter—and you're right, he's a liar too. The Inuit hate him."

"He pays them well," Commander Peary said with a frown.

"The Inuit take his money, but they laugh at him. They think he's an idiot. Why, the man hates dogs!" I laughed, but the Commander still looked grim.

In his cabin, Commander Peary had spread out his maps. He showed me the way that Dr. Cook was taking to get to the North Pole.

"See?" Peary pointed out an island to the northeast. "On paper, Cook's route looks faster." He looked up at me. "We have to make the Pole this time, Matt."

"We will, Commander. And I don't believe Dr. Cook will make it onto the ice cap, let alone as far as the Pole."

Peary smiled a little when I said that, but it was the truth. I didn't believe that man was any danger to us.

*

When we arrived in Greenland, I was heartbroken to find that Ahnalka and Ikwah had died during the time we had been home in America. But they had told their families and tribes about me. The younger Inuit respected me. And I was still the only one on our expedition who spoke their language. They gave me a new name—Mahri-Paluq, which means "the kind one."

Peary and I knew the Arctic well now. We knew this last expedition would take a year at least. Once we got to Greenland, we began to get the trail ready. In the months before the long, dark winter set in, we left our base camp and went ahead along the trail to leave food ready for the expedition. We left food that would be safe in the ice—pemmican, mostly, a mixture of fat and dried meat—and oil for cooking.

Then we returned to base camp for the winter, to wait for the return of the sun. In March, we were ready to go. Our expedition, complete with ninety-eight dogs, set off from our final camp on Cape Sheridan on the very north of Ellesmere Island.

We had a pretty good method of travel. We split into teams of three, two Inuit and one American in each team, and each team with its own dogs. The two Inuit who came with me were Ootah and Segloo. They told me their families sang songs about me—and not rude songs like the ones they sang about Dr. Cook!

After five days' trekking, we reached the camp we had prepared at Cape Columbia. From here we would make the dash to the Pole. We were leaving land and would set out across the frozen sea, sledding four hundred and thirteen miles north to the Pole.

We traveled all through March. Every night we made camp and built igloos. The weather took a turn for the worse. It was so cold our breath froze on our fur hoods. Our cheeks and noses were frozen and it was so cold it was impossible to sleep. Some of the sleds broke and I had to work in the cold to fix them.

By this time, I didn't think I had much chance of getting to the Pole. Every few days one of the teams would be sent back to base camp. We knew Commander Peary would only choose one team of the three who'd traveled this far north to make the final push to the Pole. Most of us thought Peary would chose Captain Bartlett to go with him. Captain Bartlett was the second in command and a close friend of Peary's. Everyone agreed that he would not choose me. "Why would the Commander choose a black man?" they all said. But at last, the only people left alongside Peary were Captain Bartlett, me, and the Inuit explorers.

It was hard to tell what Peary was thinking. He was gloomy and silent these days. Maybe he was thinking that this was our last chance. If we didn't make it this time, he knew he'd never get to the Pole. Whatever it was, he was less friendly, more distant. I thought he was getting ready to send me home. So when he called me into his igloo and told me he'd made his choice of partner for the final push to the Pole, my heart was in my mouth.

"Matthew," Commander Peary said. He had used my full name. That was bad news. It must mean he was sending me home. I couldn't look him in the face.

"Commander," I said. "I understand . . ." and I turned to go.

"Matt?" He stopped me from going. "I need someone I can trust completely at the Pole."

"Sir?"

Commander Peary put his hand on my arm. "I am sending Bartlett back to camp . . ."

That meant I would be the only American left with him. He had chosen me to go with him to the Pole! I could hardly speak—there was a lump in my throat the size of an egg. I nodded my thanks and took a deep breath.

"I promise, sir. I won't let you down."

And so on April 1, 1909, Captain Bartlett left to return to base camp, and Ootah, Segloo, and I set off for the North Pole. Commander Peary traveled with his team, Egingwah and Ooqueah.

My party went ahead. Truth was, the Commander couldn't go as fast, because his lack of toes meant he had to ride on the sled. So we were the ones in the lead. The plan was for us to make another camp and take the readings that told us our position. We'd build an igloo for the Commander first, and then one for us.

The ice lay in huge plates and in between were vast dark crevasses. As we pushed our way forward, I lost my footing and fell into the freezing Arctic water.

Ootah was quick as lightning. He grabbed me by the back of my jacket with both hands and hauled me out of the ice-cold water. I was shivering so hard my teeth clattered in my mouth. I was so cold it felt as if I was burning up. I lay on the ice at the edge of the water, my fur clothes heavy and freezing hard with every minute. Ootah acted fast. He quickly found me some dry furs in our pack and I warmed my feet on his stomach in the way Ahnalka had showed me.

When Peary's group caught up, Peary was riding on the sled and looked paler and older than before. He had fallen into the water too.

*

We traveled another five days. My team rode ahead of the Commander. At the end of every day's march, we built igloos and took readings to map our position. It was on April 6, late in the day, when I stopped to take the readings. My hands were frozen, even in my fur gloves, and the first time I checked the sun's position I could not believe it. I thought I must have made a mistake, so I tried again. I checked the compass too, but the needle was moving wildly. I looked at Ootah. I must have been smiling, because he gave me a look like he thought I was nuts.

"Mahri?" he said, frowning.

I checked the compass one more time.

"We made it!" I cried. "We're here! Look at the compass! We're here!"

I clapped him on the back so hard he almost fell over. "The North Pole!" I told him. "We're on the top of the world! The first men ever to stand here in all of history." My legs were so cold and worn out that I couldn't dance for joy but I was grinning and laughing and hugging Ootah.

Ootah stepped back and looked at me. "This is it? This is the place you've spent years looking for?" He looked around. "I can show you plenty of ice like this back home, Mahri-Paluq."

I smiled. Ootah laughed.

Segloo shook his head and told us to stop joking around—we still had an igloo to build.

About forty-five minutes later, we heard Commander Peary and the others arriving. I thought he'd be as excited as me, but he said nothing. I watched as he unpacked his own equipment to take more readings just to make sure. It was very hard to take readings because we were so far north, and he needed to be certain. Then Commander Peary took out an American flag from his pack.

"We will plant the Stars and Stripes at the North Pole!" he said, and I felt a real thrill of pride. We had made it! We were the first men ever to stand on the top of the world.

We only spent a day and a half at the Pole. And I must admit I thought the Commander was ill, on account of how little he said, but looking back I think Peary was angry that he hadn't been the very first one of us to reach the Pole. My team and I had gotten there before him.

We had spent over nineteen years trying to get there, but we were all so worn out. And we knew we still had the long journey back to base camp.

We traveled back as quickly as we could; in fact, we were back at base camp by the end of April and I don't think any people on Earth were more pleased than us to see our ship. I took my fur clothes off for the first time in two months and for days afterward did nothing but eat and sleep.

We stayed in the north until the sea ice began to melt in July, and it was on the 17th that we set sail for America.

When I said goodbye to our Inuit companions, Ootah asked if I would be coming back next year. I shook my head. He didn't understand. Was that it? Was that the end of our friendship? All those risks and that time together for an empty space on the ice? And now I was leaving. I tried to explain it to him. We had reached our goal, we had been the first men at the North Pole. I knew his family and the Inuit of Greenland would always be a part of me. That even though I wouldn't be back, I would never forget. Their memory would always be deep inside me.

CHAPTER 12

That last journey home was hard. On September 21, when we put into port at Indian Harbour, Nova Scotia, on the Canadian coast, there was bad news. Peary had a message. Dr. Cook had returned to New York that very same day and told everyone he was the first man to reach the North Pole. He claimed he had got there the previous year, in April 1908. He received a hero's welcome.

Peary was angry. He couldn't believe what had happened. Before we left Greenland, I had spoken to the Inuit who had traveled with Dr. Cook and they told me he hadn't gone anywhere near the Pole. Dr. Cook was lying. I tried to tell Peary this but it was no good.

He wouldn't listen to me. He had given his whole life to being the first man to reach the North Pole and now he thought we'd failed.

"The press believe Cook!" Peary said. "We're too late!"

And Commander Peary was right.

When we reached New York, a whole month later, there was no one to meet us. Commander Peary stayed in his cabin, so I went ashore to find out what had happened. I stopped a boy selling newspapers on a street corner.

"Didn't you hear?" he said. "Some fellow's already found the North Pole. He came back a few weeks ago."

"Dr. Cook?" I asked.

"That's the one," the boy said. "Should have seen the parade the city gave him—so much ticker tape they were cleaning it up for weeks afterward ..."

I bought a copy of his newspaper. Reading it only confirmed everything Commander Peary had feared. **Second Expedition Reaches the Pole!**, screamed the headline.

The report made it clear they thought it was impossible that Peary, with only four Inuit and a colored man to help him, could have made it to the North Pole.

If he'd really made it, the newspaper said, why didn't he take any of the white explorers? Why didn't he take the scientists or Navy men?

And anyway, Peary's expedition didn't matter one bit because the famous Dr. Cook had already claimed the North Pole.

I crumpled up the newspaper and tossed it in the rubbish. Had I forgotten what it was like away from the ice? There were still a lot of people in the United States of America who thought we colored folk didn't count. They thought that a man like me wouldn't survive a journey to the Pole. That I couldn't know how to drive dogs or survive intense cold.

I knew there was nothing I could do. I had to find work, look after myself. My life of discovery and exploration was over. I'm sad to say that Commander Peary never got in touch with me again. I think he held it against me that my party reached the Pole first, but I can never be sure. I would have liked the chance to talk to him—after all, we had shared so much danger and excitement. But it never happened.

CHAPTER 13

I stayed on in New York and found work. It was only parking cars, and I thought sadly of all that Captain Childs had said to me many years ago. There was not much money, but it was regular work. I often thought that if I told the people around me how I'd spent my life exploring the Arctic ice cap, they would just have looked at me as if I was making it all up— the way people had looked at Baltimore Jack.

But one day, as I waited to park some rich folks' car, I saw Dr. Cook's name in big letters across a newspaper. **Dr. Frederick Cook a Liar!!** I picked up the paper and read. Why— the man wasn't even a doctor. He'd begun life as a milkman in Brooklyn, a suburb of

New York. And, just like the Inuit said, his expedition hadn't got anywhere near the Pole. The newspaper wrote about another expedition Dr. Cook had claimed to have made where he'd said he'd climbed one of the biggest mountains in America. It turned out that he'd faked the photographs.

I grinned to myself. Ootah and Segloo and I, we had been the first men at the Pole after all!

*

In 1910, the American government announced that our expedition was the first true journey to the North Pole. Commander Peary was promoted to Admiral and made a member of the Explorers' Club. The President gave him a medal too. He gave medals to all the other white members of the expedition. But not me. They wouldn't even let me join their club.

I knew there was nothing I could do, even if we black people worked three times as hard. I knew life was not fair.

Even if white folk in America did not want to know about me, I reckoned there might still be some people who did. I had taken a lot of photographs of our travels, so I toured the colored universities and made a little money giving talks and showing the photos.

Three more years passed, and in 1913 the President's office sent me a telegram with the offer of a job working for the government. I expect the government thought that since I'd been to the North Pole and planted the Stars and Stripes at the top of the world it owed me something. I was nearly fifty years old and the job was only working as a messenger. Once again I was called a "boy" but I was glad of the work. The money was regular and it was better than parking cars.

Admiral Peary died in 1920. He had a hero's funeral—full military honors. I read about it in the newspapers but no one invited me. Admiral Peary had never contacted me after our last trip. That made me very sad but I had to live in the present. I always knew life would be different for me. I was colored. But I knew that I had done great things. I had learned so much, seen so much.

When I was sixty-one, the government gave me a new, better job. At last I was a clerk and I could sit down in an office.

Slowly, America began to change. In 1937, the Explorers' Club invited me to join—the first colored member they ever had. I still didn't get the top medal, but in 1944 the president decided I could have a special Peary Polar Expedition Medal and he gave it to me himself.

Who would have thought it? A colored man, an orphan beaten and homeless, with no money in his pocket and no shoes on his feet, working since the age of eleven, at last had the honor and thanks of the whole country.

One thing I knew for certain. Captain Childs would have been proud of me then.

Our books are tested
for children and young people by
children and young people.

Thanks to everyone who consulted on
a manuscript for their time and effort in
helping us to make our books better
for our readers.